Okinawa Diet

A Beginner's 3-Week Step-by-Step Guide With Curated Recipes and a 7-Day Meal Plan

BRUCE ACKERBERG

Disclaimer

By reading this disclaimer, you are accepting the terms of the disclaimer in full. If you disagree with this disclaimer, please do not read the guide.

All of the content within this guide is provided for informational and educational purposes only, and should not be accepted as independent medical or other professional advice. The author is not a doctor, physician, nurse, mental health provider, or registered nutritionist/dietician. Therefore, using and reading this guide does not establish any form of a physician-patient relationship.

Always consult with a physician or another qualified health provider with any issues or questions you might have regarding any sort of medical condition. Do not ever disregard any qualified professional medical advice or delay seeking that advice because of anything you have read in this guide. The information in this guide is not intended to be any sort of medical advice and should not be used in lieu of any medical advice by a licensed and qualified medical professional.

The information in this guide has been compiled from a variety of known sources. However, the author cannot attest to or guarantee the accuracy of each source and thus should not be held liable for any errors or omissions.

Introduction

Do you want to live a longer life? Without cashing out money on high-end expensive treatments? Newly formulated products? Or regular therapeutic trips to different commercial spaces? If you think it seems impossible, well, think again as you are about to know the secret to having a longer life!

According to the United Nations, the global average life expectancy rose to its peak of 72.6 years old in 2019. 1 This is by far the longest life expectancy that we have achieved after 1950. In line with this, some areas in the world still live a longer life expectancy than most places. These are called blue zones. 2

These blue zones are areas that hold different lifestyles and cultures that are unique only to them, And their practices are said to be connected to having higher life expectancy.

One of these blue zones is Okinawa in Japan, a region that houses the longest-lived women in the world. In fact, for every 100,000 inhabitants in this region, there are 68 centenarians, or people who live at least 100 years old. Also, Japan is the second country that has the highest life expectancy in the world with 84.67 years old in 2019.

Okinawans credit their longevity to a mantra from Confucius that is recited before meals "Hara hachi bu." This mantra always prompts them to stop eating when they are almost full, thus, preventing themselves from overeating. Also, they are family-oriented people and implied that living longer would make them feel more accomplished in life.

So, what if I told you that one of the secrets of the longevity of the Okinawans is their diet? And that you will find out about their secret diet in this guide.

In the following guide, you will discover…

- What the "Okinawa diet" is
- How to eat like an Okinawan
- How to live like the Okinawans
- How to plan meals as if you are Okinawan
- How to maintain the Okinawan lifestyle

Table of Contents

ABOUT THE OKINAWAN DIET

The Okinawa Diet is the traditional diet of the residents in Okinawa, Japan, who are known to have a longer average life expectancy compared with most areas in the world. A lot of the residents here reach a hundred years old, boasting healthy bodies and a low risk of diseases associated with age.

It is said that this longer-than-average life expectancy is brought by their lifestyle, particularly their diets, which consist of nutritionally dense yet low-calorie foods. Their diet also includes food that is rich in antioxidants and flavonoids that aid in preventing the development of cancer.

Moreover, research implies that diets resulting in reduced risk of developing chronic diseases (like the Okinawa diet) tend to be heavy on vegetables, and at the same time, consume less meat, saturated fat, refined grains, salt, sugar, and fatty dairy products. The Okinawa diet shares similar characteristics with the DASH (Dietary Approaches to Stop Hypertension) diet and the Mediterranean diet--- diets that are scientifically proven to be healthy.

What can you get from following the Okinawan diet?

Because the diet consists mainly of low-calorie yet nutrient-dense food, people doing the Okinawan diet tend to have lower risks of developing some kinds of cancer, cardiovascular diseases, and chronic diseases, and less oxidative stress that pressures their cells to degenerate more quickly. To be more specific, here are possible health benefits of following the Okinawa diet:

- **Reduced risk of developing chronic diseases**

The Okinawa diet features traditional food from Okinawa that is high in fiber, macronutrients, micronutrients, and phytonutrients while being low in refined sugar, saturated fats, and of course, calories.

One food that is heavily recommended in this diet is sweet potatoes. Sweet potatoes are a star in the Okinawa diet because this food is said to contain the right amount of fiber and with a low glycemic index (GI), which means that it is safer for diabetic people because foods with a low glycemic index (GI) do not cause sharp rises in one's blood glucose. Sweet potatoes also contain essential micronutrients such as potassium, magnesium, calcium, retinol (vitamin A), and ascorbic acid (vitamin C).

In addition to sweet potatoes, various vegetables—especially the colorful ones—that are consumed in the Okinawan diet are also deemed healthy because of the presence of carotenoid in these foods, an antioxidant-containing compound that offers anti-inflammatory effects that help in preventing the development of type 2 diabetes and heart diseases.

Furthermore, the Okinawa diet also includes the consumption of soy, which is a great component of foods related to a decreased risk of developing chronic diseases such as cancer and heart disease. Soy is also one of the protein sources in diets that require limited to prohibited consumption of animal protein such as in strict vegan diets.

- **Increased life expectancy**

Of course, this diet is known as the diet of Okinawans who tend to have higher average life longevity than other parts of the world.

A study revealed that Okinawa is the home of more people who are at least a hundred years old, all thanks to their genetics and lifestyle.

Although the relationship between the Okinawa Diet and longevity is often connected, there are not enough studies to support this claim because there are lots of factors that affect longevity other than lifestyle. This includes the environment and genetics. Another factor would be high amounts of free radicals which can bring stress, resulting in cellular damage in the body that may speed up aging, thus, eventually, affecting longevity. Consequently, this stress brought by free radicals may be countered by compounds called antioxidants that protect the cells from being damaged. These antioxidants are highly present in various vegetables and root crops—all abundant in the traditional Okinawa diet.

Moreover, animal studies have revealed that diets with restricted caloric intake promote a longer lifespan compared with Western diets that are high in protein. Because diets similar to the Okinawa diet are high in carbohydrates, low in protein, and low in calories, they may also promote a longer lifespan.

How do Okinawans eat?

It has been constantly reiterated that the Okinawa diet is high in carbohydrates, low in protein, and low in saturated fats, refined sugar, and calories. So, in this diet, the aim is to consume nutrient-dense food that is low in calories as much as possible. To help you visualize how Okinawans eat, the following are food groups that are included in this diet, listed with sample foods.

- An abundance of vegetables and root crops such as bamboo shoots, bitter melon, cabbage, carrots, Chinese okra, daikon radish, green papaya, kelp, orange sweet potato, pumpkin, purple sweet potato, seaweed, and squash

- A portion of grains like rice, noodles, millet, and wheat. These can be whole or milled, but it is important to note that whole grains contain more fiber and nutrients.

- A few soy-based foods such as miso, edamame, natto, and tofu.

- Minimal amounts of meat and seafood (wherein fish with white meat is preferred), other seafood, and occasional consumption of pork (including the organs). When choosing protein sources, low-fat meats are recommended.

- Jasmine tea, spices (such as turmeric), alcohol (sake), and broth (dashi) are also taken minimally.

In summary, the Okinawa diet consists of nutrient-rich foods that are low in calories. Plant-based foods also make up most of the diet because these foods are high in fiber, antioxidants, anti-inflammatory compounds, and essential nutrients. These whole foods are also not difficult to obtain because the Okinawa prefecture is fit for the farming and livestock industry due to its subtropical climate. They also manufacture goods that are shipped to other countries.

What do Okinawans avoid eating?

If Okinawans are very particular about what they eat, it is also right for them to be mindful of what they SHOULD NOT eat.

The foods listed below that are not recommended in the diet are also the same foods that are not very accessible to them. So, their geography also took part in their eating habits. Thus, the traditional Okinawan Diet tells us to avoid:

- Meats like poultry, beef, and processed ones such as bacon, hotdogs, ham, sausage, salami, chorizo, pepperoni, pastrami, and other cured meat.
- Animal products such as eggs and dairy products like butter, cheese, milk, and yogurt.
- Other processed foods like cereals, refined grains, refined sugar, processed snacks, and cooking oil from animal fat.

- Legumes such as chickpeas, lentils, beans, peas, seeds, and nuts except for soybeans
- Other food items like most fruits and their seeds

The items above are the foods to be avoided when under the traditional Okinawan diet. But they may be consumed minimally in the modern version because it only considers the caloric content of foods. For example, foods with lower calories may be allowed—such as fruits. However, it is still advised that foods with high caloric content like seeds, nuts, and dairy products should still be consumed minimally.

THE OKINAWAN WAY: EASY OR DIFFICULT?

You have already been informed about the benefits of following the Okinawan way. But, just like other diets, the Okinawa diet also has possible downsides. It may be restrictive for some, difficult to execute, or just not fit for the budget. To be more elaborate, listed below are some factors to consider before doing a full-on diet:

- **Excludes different food groups.** The Okinawa diet is quite restrictive when it comes to food allowed for consumption. In this diet, calories are low, thus, it may not be suitable for people with active lifestyles such as athletes and blue-collared job workers because these people require more energy than other people.

And as a rule of thumb, it is not always ideal to have very low amounts of protein in the diet because it is essential for the growth, development, and recovery of the muscles. Also, the Okinawa diet restricts the consumption of seeds, nuts, fruits, and dairy--- all good sources of essential micronutrients such as protein and fat, in addition to vitamins, minerals, fiber, and antioxidants that may also improve health.

- Availability of foods. If you are living in the city, where fresh whole foods are expensive, and sometimes not at all fresh, it may be difficult to achieve this diet because of the limited items that can be found in your area. You may always choose to grow your food, but this will be difficult if you do not have a backyard, a lawn, or even a balcony where you can plant your feet.
- The Okinawa diet may be high in sodium. The Okinawa diet has different versions, some of which include the traditional and the modern versions.

Ironically, despite the Okinawa diet being advertised to reduce the risk of developing cardiovascular diseases, some versions of this diet give out as much as 3,200 milligrams of sodium per day, which is not at all appropriate for people with hypertension because this amount of sodium may endanger their cardiovascular health. The American Heart Association recommends a 1,500 mg per day limit for hypertensive people, while a 2,300 mg limit for people with normal blood pressure.

However, the Okinawa diet may also potentially display high amounts of potassium which counterbalances the effect of high sodium in the body. The adequate amount of potassium in our body encourages the kidneys to remove extra fluid, thus, reducing blood pressure and further flushing away excess sodium.

A little tip if you are hypertensive and want to try the Okinawa diet: Just avoid the high-sodium foods in the diet such as broth.

HOW TO LIVE LIKE THE OKINAWANS (WEEK 1)

In the past few chapters, you learned what the Okinawa Diet is all about, what foods to consume, and what to avoid. At this point, you may have already weighed the pros and cons of this diet and are curious to know how to start it.

In this chapter, you will get to know the Okinawans' way of living in terms of their diet and lifestyle. To head start this journey, you should remember the following tips on your first week of the diet.

- **Declutter**

You are about to change your habits to better ones. So, you should not let your old habits control you. Learn to declutter, not only physical items such as food items in the "To Avoid" section but also your old bad habits. Do you often eat bacon and eggs for breakfast? Maybe it is time to toss this habit away and try to go for a more Okinawan option such as a mixed vegetable salad that is palatable, refreshing, and low in calories. However, if you are still not ready to get rid of your old habits, you can always take it slowly. In this case, you may eat your bacon and eggs today, add some vegetables or grains, and eliminate either the bacon or eggs tomorrow, until you have completely "decluttered" those bad habits.

Decluttering is important because having constant reminders of your old habits may lead you to go back to them, eventually, leaving you to start over. So, it would be nice to see everything on a clean slate to have a fresh Okinawan start.

- **Take it lightly**

Lifestyle changes such as diet shifts are not a process that will take you a day. It is a constant change and habits should be established. So, do not pressure yourself to eat what you cannot eat at the moment because this will only give a negative connotation to the diet that you are trying to do. Instead, understand, be patient, and be disciplined with the starting process.

- **Fill the empty**

Since you have already decluttered (or are still in the process), it is time to feel the emptiness of having your old habits thrown out. Fill this gap with new habits that you are about to learn at the start of your journey. This includes:

- o Preparing a grocery list that consists of food items in the "To Eat" section of the Okinawa diet
- o Keeping a diary where you can write your Okinawa diet journey
- o Learning how to cook your meals
- o Trying to prepare a week's meal plan

o Familiarizing yourself with healthier Okinawan substitutes to your old-time favorites
o Learning Okinawan ways in the different aspects of life

In addition to your own independent life, did you know that Okinawans like to socialize? They meet in groups and talk about different things. And if a member of their group did not show up, a portion of the group dresses up and goes around the village to check on the missing member.

You can also apply this during your first week. You can look for communities that do the Okinawan diet. They may be a local club or organization, or even online communities where you can freely share your concerns about the diet. In this way, you will be immersed with people who have been at your place, therefore, you have someone to relate to and seek help from.

Since you are still starting, here is a sample 7-day meal plan that you can easily follow.

	Breakfast	Lunch	Snack	Dinner
Monday	Carrot fry	Okinawan Shoyu Pork	Milk from Soybeans	Stir-fried bamboo, bitter melon, and cabbage
Tuesday	Turmeric Tea	Easy Okinawan Taco Rice Recipe	Vegetable Salad with Vinaigrette Dressing	Vegetable Stew with Miso Soup
Wednesday	Sticky Rice	Okinawa Soba	Soybean curd with vanilla and sweet potato starch pearls	Stir-fried papaya with ground lean pork
Thursday	Tofu and Vegetable	Smoked Salmon	Mushroom soup	Steamed sweet potatoes
Friday	Jasmine Tea	Seasoned Chicken Breast in Chicken Broth	Soybean milk	Stir-fried broccoli
Saturday	Apple Shake with Quinoa Seeds and honey	Sashimi and Rice	Seaweed and vegetable salad	Soybean and lentils with squash and spinach
Sunday	Jasmine Tea	California Maki	Fried sweet potato fries in vegetable oil	Stir-fried marinated seaweeds with tofu

HOW TO PLAN YOUR MEALS LIKE THE OKINAWANS (WEEK 2)

The first week may be a difficult one. But with determination and will, things will eventually get better. In the second week, you must redo the things you have done in the first week and familiarize yourself with the general guidelines of the diet.

This time is like your second test run and your actual application of the things you have learned. To help you get through, here are some tips that you may follow in your second week:

- Note the things you think you are doing wrong and consult helpful sources. Do not be afraid to seek advice if things do not go as planned and expected.

- Keep things right and on track by regularly updating your diary. You can jot down what you eat, and what you do for physical activities, and maybe, track your inventory so you know what to consume first and what items to buy. By keeping a diary, you can see how you improve through the days which will give you a sense of achievement.

- Explore the grocery store for more options other than what you are used to. You may be on your way to another day of grocery shopping, and you may have written a list. But be open also to new products such as vegetables you have not tried before. Or grains that are foreign to you. This diet may not only be a journey for yourself but for your taste buds as well.

- Do not be afraid to experiment. In diets where you are encouraged to cook, one of the best experiences would be creating a dish from all your favorites. You may be following foolproof recipes already, but this does not mean that you are limited to only using these. Be confident and release the inner chef in you! This makes the journey more fun because you are learning new skills every day.

Speaking of meals and cooking below is another 7-day meal plan that could help you visualize how you should eat. Remember that you are not restricted to only eating meals listed on the table. Just like the tip in the first week, familiarize yourself with possible substitutes so that you can have a variety of meals every day.

	Breakfast	**Lunch**	**Snack**	**Dinner**
Monday	Sweet potato fry	Stir-fried brown rice and hijiki	Choice Tea	Stir-fried bamboo, bitter melon, and cabbage
Tuesday	Tofu and Mashed sweet potatoes scramble	Sushi rolls	Soybean curd with vanilla and sweet potato starch pearls	Hawaiian Ahi Poke
Wednesday	Miso soup	Stir-fried bok-choy with Japanese Soba noodles	Vegetable Salad with Vinaigrette Dressing	Stir-fried papaya with ground lean pork
Thursday	Natto congee	Fried salmon with brown rice	Mushroom soup	Teriyaki Tofu fries
Friday	Turmeric Tea	Seasoned Chicken Breast in Chicken Broth	Seaweed and vegetable salad	Japanese Soba Salad with Spinach and Seaweeds
Saturday	Congee	Sashimi and Rice	Soybean milk	Soybean and lentils with squash and spinach
Sunday	Jasmine Tea	Sushi Rolls	Carrot fry	Tsumire Soup with Tofu

HOW TO KEEP YOUR OKINAWAN LIFESTYLE AT ITS BEST

As expected, you are already in your third week. It is expected that you have established your foundation on an Okinawan diet, and you can even pick out Okinawan food items in the grocery store with your eyes closed! Whether you are at this point or still going there, your efforts are already commendable because you have already reached the third week.

At this point, you may have already rid some of your previous habits of a bad lifestyle and you are almost full-on Okinawa in terms of diet. Before this guide ends, we will leave you the following tips:

- Maintain good habits. Nothing is more bummer than starting good habits and then completely forgetting them once you have achieved your goal. Always remember that is a never-ending process, thus, you should always maintain the good habits you have already worked hard for in starting.

- Be disciplined. Remember your first weeks in the diary? If you read it and realize how much you have improved, you will most likely not want to come back to your old ways. So, learn how to control yourself from steering back to your old ways.
- Keep your goals in mind. Whether your goal is to lose weight, start a healthier lifestyle, or have a longer life, keep these goals in mind as these will be your driving force.

The Okinawa diet may be the change you are looking for to achieve your goal. At this moment, you may have already figured out how it is properly done, and if it is right for you. If the diet suits you, then you deserve to achieve your goals with it. If it is not, then you still deserve to be congratulated for trying your best and reaching this stage.

The Okinawa diet, whether it does indeed help for longevity or not, is overall a good diet that is practiced by the Okinawans. So, following it may give you the benefits mentioned in the earlier chapters and the chance to embody the Okinawans' way of living. This journey will not only change your lifestyle but will also teach you the culture of Okinawans and appreciate it.

To end this guide below is a sample meal plan you can surely achieve and might recreate.

	Breakfast	Lunch	Snack	Dinner
Monday	Sweet potato fry	Sashimi on steamed brown rice with soy sauce	Soybean curd with vanilla and sweet potato starch pearls	Tofu and Mushroom Steak marinated in Sake paired with brown rice
Tuesday	Pickled vegetables and tempura	Soba salad with green vegetables	Seaweed and vegetable salad	Shiitake Mushrooms and Potato Soup with Tomatoes and Okra
Wednesday	Nori Rolls	Papaya, Bean Sprouts, and Vegetable Rolls	Turmeric Tea	Okinawan Sweet Potato Soup
Thursday	Seafood Miso soup paired with Steamed Brown Rice	Baked and Salted Sweet Potato	Mushroom soup	Sauteed mushrooms with brown rice
Friday	Soy and Spinach with Brown Rice Porridge	Vegetarian Soba with Cabbage, Radish, and tofu	Seaweed and vegetable salad	Stir-fried fish tofu and asparagus
Saturday	Miso soup with tofu and spinach	Sweet potato soup with steamed brown rice	Jasmine Tea	Darjeeling rice pudding with Mixed vegetable Soup
Sunday	Grilled scad with white radish bits and brown rice	Stir-fried bean sprouts in rice wraps	Green Tea	Mochi and Tofu dumplings

CURATED RECIPES

Stir-Fried Carrots

Ingredients:

- 3 carrots, peeled and julienned
- 1 egg, whisked
- 1 tsp. soy sauce
- 1 tsp. sesame oil
- 1 5-oz. tuna canned tuna in oil
- salt
- pepper
- water
- 1 green onion, for garnish

Instructions:

1. Over medium-high heat, put on a skillet. Put the oil from the tuna and heat it up.
2. Stir fry the carrots until softened, about 10 minutes. Pour a bit of water if needed.
3. Add half a can of tuna, followed by sesame oil and soy sauce, then season with pepper and salt.
4. Pour the whisked egg while stirring nonstop.

5. Remove from heat. Garnish with green onion and serve immediately.

Tofu and Vegetables

Ingredients:

- 1 cup carrots, sliced
- 1 12-14-oz. tofu, packaged firm in water, cut into small cubes
- 2 cups white or yellow onion, sliced
- 1 tbsp. butter
- 1-2 tbsp. olive oil
- 1-2 bunch green onions, white and green parts sliced
- 2 tbsp. soy sauce
- fresh ground pepper
- salt
- sesame seeds, for garnish

Instructions:

1. Prep a pan for frying or sautéing by heating it up over medium to medium-high heat.
2. Heat up the butter in the pan until melted.
3. Slowly add carrots and white or yellow onion to stir fry for 3-4 minutes. Season with salt and pepper.
4. Transfer to a plate and set aside.
5. Toss the tofu in the pan for about 3-4 minutes. Do it just about once or twice.
6. Pour in soy sauce, followed by the veggies. Heat for about a minute then shut it off.

7. Garnish with green onions and sesame seeds.

Okinawan Shoyu Pork

Ingredients:

- 1/2 cup of soy sauce
- 1-1/2 lb. whole pork belly
- 1/2 cup mirin
- 2 tsp. ground ginger
- 1/2 cup of water
- 1 clove garlic, or to taste
- 1/2 cup packed brown sugar

Instructions:

1. In a large pot, place the pork belly with water, covering up to about an inch over the pork.
2. Place the pot over medium-high heat to simmer for a couple of minutes.
3. Throw away boiled water and replace it with fresh one, with the same amount.
4. Allow again to boil on medium-high heat, then leave it to simmer over low heat. Cook until the pork softens.
5. Get the pork from the pot for cutting.
6. Chop the meat to about an inch wide.
7. In a large saucepan, mix the brown sugar, garlic, ginger, mirin, soy sauce, and a half cup of water. Fire up the heat and bring it to a boil.
8. Put the pork belly, and leave to boil.
9. Lower the heat then place an aluminum foil sheet over the meat and sauce.

10. Leave it to simmer without the pot's cover for about 30-45 minutes.

11. Make sure to repeatedly flip over the pork while simmering.

Okinawan Taco

Ingredients:

- 1 egg
- 1 tomato, chopped
- 1/2 cup cheese
- 5 iceberg lettuce, chopped

Cauliflower Rice:

- 2 cups cauliflower rice
- 1/2 tsp. salt
- 2 tbsp. olive oil
- 1/2 tsp. cumin powder
- 1/2 tsp. garlic powder
- 1/2 tsp. onion powder

Taco Meat:

- 1/2 lb. ground beef
- 1/2 red pepper, diced
- 1/4 onion, diced
- 3/4 tsp. cumin
- 1/2 tsp. chili powder

- 1.25 tsp. garlic powder
- 1/4 tsp. onion powder
- 1/4 tsp. paprika powder
- 2 tbsp. olive oil
- 1 tsp. salt
- 1.5 tsp. oregano
- 1/2 cup water
- 1 tbsp. tomato paste

Instructions:

1. In a frying pan over medium heat, pour the olive oil to stir fry red pepper and onion until softened.
2. Put the ground meat. Cook for a couple of minutes.
3. Then, add the spices, followed by water. Cook until water has evaporated, about 3-4 minutes. Then, set it aside.
4. Using the same pan over medium heat, cook the egg sunny side up while covered, for a couple of minutes.
5. On a frying pan—you can use the same one—pour the oil, followed by the cauliflower rice and spices to cook for no more than 5 minutes.
6. Serve everything on a large plate. First, put the cauliflower rice, then cover it with lettuce and stir-fried meat, then top off with cheese, tomato, and fried egg.

Turmeric Tea

Ingredients:

- 1/4 tsp. turmeric powder

- 1 cup milk
- 1 tsp. honey

Instructions:

1. Heat up the milk, but no need to boil it.
2. In a cup, put the turmeric followed by the heated milk.
3. Stir well before covering. Allow this to steep for 5 minutes before adding the honey.

Okinawan Braised Pork

Ingredients:

- 30g kiriboshi daikon, soaked in water and later drained
- 150g pork belly, cut into small strips
- 20g carrot, shredded thinly
- 30g dried kombu kelp, shredded, rinsed, and drained
- 1 handful skipjack shavings
- 1 tbsp. sesame oil
- 2 tbsp. soy sauce
- 2 tbsp. raw sugar
- 300 ml. water

Instructions:

1. Briefly blanch the pork in hot water.
2. Prepare a nonwoven spice bag to put the skipjack shavings in.

3. In a pot with a tablespoon of sesame oil, gently stir-fry pork, along with kombu and kiriboshi daikon.
4. Add the sugar, followed by the spice bag and water, then leave it to boil.
5. Pour the soy sauce. Lower the heat and use a drop lid to cover.
6. Leave to simmer for about half an hour.
7. Remove the spice bag then stir in the carrots. Simmer again for 30 minutes.

Okinawa Soba

Ingredients:

- 7 oz. Okinawa soba noodles, cooked according to instructions
- 2 lbs. pork belly
- 200 ml sake or awamori
- 1 green onion, chopped
- 100 ml soy sauce
- 400 ml water
- 4 tbsp. mirin
- 1/2 cup sugar
- 3 pcs. ginger slices
- 2 tbsp. honey

Dashi:

- 1L Water
- a handful of bonito flakes
- 2 tbsp. soy sauce

- 1 tsp. salt
- 2 tsp. sugar

Pickled ginger:

- 100g ginger, sliced thinly
- 100ml sushi vinegar
- 100ml rice vinegar

Instructions:

1. In a pressure cooker, put the pork belly and cover it with enough water. Heat it up.
2. When it starts to pressurize, lower the heat and simmer for about 20 minutes.
3. Remove the cooker from the heat and allow it to cool down before opening. Run under tap water to speed up the cooling process.
4. Get the pork belly to wash it in water. After doing so, slice up the pork to about 3-cm. thick.
5. Put the pork back in the newly rinsed pressure cooker, followed by sugar, soy sauce, mirin, honey, ginger, awamori, and water. Allow it to pressurize, then lower the heat and leave it to simmer for about 10 more minutes.

For the pickled ginger:

Mix the sushi vinegar and rice vinegar with the ginger to marinate it. Leave for about 15 minutes, until it turns pale pink.

For the soup and serving:

1. Boil a liter of water, then move it away from the fire.
2. Put the bonito flakes in the water. Leave it to steep for a minute or two.
3. To make the dashi, strain the flakes, then add salt, sugar, and soy sauce to the dashi.
4. Put the drained noodles in bowls. Pour over the soup and top with the pork, pickled ginger, and green onion. Serve while hot.

Sticky Rice

Ingredients:

- 1-1/4 cups water
- 2 cups mochiko or sticky rice flour
- 1/4 cup water
- 1 cup sugar
- 1 tsp. coconut extract

Instructions:

1. In a mixing bowl, mix water and mochiko using a wooden spoon until you form a dough.
2. Prepare a triple cheesecloth or a thin dish towel that has been wet to put the dough in.
3. Place this in a steamer and steam for about 30-40 minutes. Then transfer to a bowl.
4. Prepare the syrup by putting water and sugar in the pot.

5. Pour the syrup into the dough.
6. Dust an 8-inch pan with flour before spreading the dough with a wet spatula.
7. Leave it overnight with a dry dish towel as a cover.
8. Use a plastic or wooden knife dipped in water to cut the rice.

Seared Salmon

Ingredients:

- 1-1/2 tbsp. canola oil
- 4 pcs. salmon filets, each filet about 1-inch thick
- 1 tsp. kosher salt
- 1 tsp. ground black pepper, 1 teaspoon
- 2/3 cups shallots, thinly sliced, 2/3 cup
- 3 cups cherry tomatoes, 3 cups
- 2 tbsp. balsamic vinegar
- 1/2 cup basil leaves, torn

Instructions:

1. Preheat the oven to 500°F.
2. Use foil when lining a rimmed baking sheet, then set aside.
3. Put a tablespoon of canola oil in a large heavy-bottomed pan placed over high heat.
4. Sprinkle evenly half of the pepper and salt over the fish filets.
5. Cook the filets in the pan for 4 minutes until the sides are golden brown.

6. Transfer the filets, with seared sides up, onto the prepared baking sheet.
7. Put it in the oven and cook the filet for about 4 minutes or until you get the degree of doneness that you prefer.
8. Return the skillet to the stove, and add the remaining canola oil.
9. Add the shallots and sauté for a couple of minutes. Season with the remaining salt and pepper.
10. Add the cherry tomatoes and 1/3 cup basil. Cook until the tomatoes are soft, for about 2 minutes.
11. Add the balsamic vinegar. Stir and cook for about a minute.
12. Transfer the filets to a serving dish and top them with the balsamic vinegar-tomato mixture. Garnish with the remaining basil.
13. Serve and enjoy while hot.

Seaweed Salad

Ingredients:

- 4 tsp. fish sauce
- 2 oz. dried seaweed such as wakame, arame, dulse, or agar
- 2 green onions, finely chopped
- 1 tsp. fresh ginger juice
- 2 tbsp. coconut water vinegar
- 2 tsp. honey
- 2 cups cucumber, finely sliced
- 1/4 cup fresh lemon juice
- 2 cups daikon radish or Japanese turnip, finely sliced

Instructions:

1. Mix together the honey, coconut water vinegar, lemon juice, fish sauce, and ginger juice to create a salad dressing.
2. Immerse the seaweed in cold water for at least 5 minutes, or until it is adequately soft.
3. Rinse and drain after. Chop if the pieces are too big.
4. Combine the rehydrated seaweed with turnips, radish, cucumber, and dressing.
5. Top with green onions as a garnish.
6. Serve and enjoy.

Tofu Hot Pot

Ingredients:

- 2 tsp. canola oil
- 6 cloves garlic, minced
- 14 oz. firm tofu, preferably water-packed, cut into 1" cubes
- 1 cup reduced-sodium soy sauce
- 1 tbsp. brown sugar
- 4 cups tender bok choy greens, sliced thinly
- 1/2 cup fresh cilantro, chopped
- 8 oz. fresh lo mein or Chinese-style noodles
- 4 oz. fresh shiitake mushrooms, stemmed and sliced
- 4 cups vegetable broth, or reduced-sodium chicken broth
- 2 tsp. chili garlic sauce, to taste

- 2 tbsp. fresh ginger, grated

Instructions:

1. In a Dutch oven over medium heat, add oil.
2. Add ginger and garlic. Stir while cooking until fragrant.
3. Add mushrooms and cook until slightly soft, about 2 to 3 minutes.
4. Stir in sugar, broth, soy sauce, and chili garlic sauce.
5. Cover and leave to boil.
6. Put in the tofu and bok choy.
7. Cover and let it simmer to cook the greens well.
8. Raise heat to high and add noodles, pushing them down into the broth.
9. Cook covered until the noodles are tender, 2 to 3 minutes.
10. Remove from the heat and stir in cilantro.
11. Serve while hot.

***Chili-garlic sauce is a spicy blend of chili, garlic, and other seasonings. It is found in the Asian section of the market.**

Smoky Cauliflower

Ingredients:

- 1 large head of cauliflower, cut into 1" florets
- 1 tsp. smoked paprika
- 2 minced garlic cloves
- 2 tbsp. fresh parsley, minced
- 2 tbsp. olive oil

- 3/4 tsp. salt

Instructions:

1. Put cauliflower inside a huge bowl.
2. In a separate bowl, combine paprika, salt, and oil.
3. Pour over cauliflower to coat.
4. Transfer to a baking pan to bake for 10 minutes, uncovered.
5. Mix in garlic.
6. Bake until cauliflower is lightly browned and tender, stirring occasionally.
7. Top with parsley upon serving.

Marinated Tuna Steak

Ingredients:

- 4 slices tuna steak
- 1/3 cup soy sauce
- 1 tbsp. cider vinegar
- 3 tbsp. olive oil
- 2 tbsp. parsley, chopped
- 1 tbsp. rosemary, chopped
- 1/2 tsp. oregano, chopped
- 1/8 tsp. garlic powder

Instructions:

1. Put together olive oil, soy sauce, parsley, cider vinegar, rosemary, and oregano in a bowl. Mix well to create a marinade mixture.
2. Using a gallon plastic bag, put tuna steaks and marinade mixture. Allow the mixture to coat the tuna by turning the bag over.
3. Leave inside the refrigerator for 30 minutes.
4. Put a small amount of oil on the grill grate. Cook tuna for about 5 minutes per side.
5. Put some of the remaining marinade mixtures on the tuna every few minutes.

Chicken Salad

Ingredients:

- 1 small can of premium chunk chicken breast packed in water
- 1 stalk celery, large, finely chopped
- 1/4 cup reduced-fat mayonnaise
- 4 romaine leaves or red leaf lettuce, washed and trimmed
- 8 pcs. cherry tomatoes or 1 ripe tomato, quartered
- 1 cucumber, small and sliced thinly

Instructions:

1. Drain canned chicken and transfer to a bowl.
2. Put in celery and mayonnaise.
3. Mix lightly. Don't crush the chicken.
4. In a separate shallow bowl, place the lettuce neatly.
5. Add the chicken salad in the middle

6. Add tomatoes and cucumber slices to the plate.
7. Refrigerate before serving, cover with plastic wrap.

Chicken Soup

Ingredients:

- 4 cups low-sodium, fat-free chicken broth
- 2 cups skinless and organic chicken, boiled and diced
- 2 carrots, diced
- 1 red onion, chopped
- 3/4 cup turnip, diced
- 1/2 cup fresh parsley, chopped

Instructions:

1. Using medium heat, boil the chicken broth in a large saucepan.
2. Add the carrots, onion, turnip, and parsley to the broth.
3. Reduce the heat from medium to low. Cover the saucepan.
4. Simmer until the vegetables are tender.
5. Add the diced chicken.
6. Simmer the soup for another 3 to 4 minutes.
7. Serve and enjoy while hot.

Turmeric Tea

Ingredients:

- 1/2 tsp. of turmeric

- 1/4 tsp. finely chopped ginger or ginger powder
- 1 cup almond milk
- 1 tsp. honey
- 1 tsp. cinnamon

Instructions:

1. Microwave almond milk for 3 minutes.
2. Stir in the ginger, cinnamon, and turmeric.
3. Drizzle honey.
4. Serve and enjoy.

Ginger Root Tea

Ingredients:

- 2 tbsp. fresh, raw ginger roots
- 2 tbsp. pure honey
- 2 cups of water
- 1 tbsp. fresh lime of lime juice

Instructions:

1. Peel and slice ginger roots thinly.
2. Boil water and add sliced ginger. Boil for 20 minutes.
3. Pour into a mug.
4. Add the lime juice and honey then mix well.
5. Drink immediately.

Broccoli Soup with Turmeric and Ginger

Ingredients:

- 1 onion
- 3 cloves garlic
- 1 can unsweetened coconut milk
- 1 tsp. salt
- 1 tsp. turmeric powder
- 2 tsp. fresh ginger chopped
- 2 small heads of broccoli chopped into florets
- 1 cup of water
- Optional, for serving: fresh greens, roasted almonds, sesame seeds, and/or yogurt

Instructions:

1. In a pan over low heat, pour half of the coconut milk.
2. Add the garlic and onion. Cook until soft, for about 5 minutes.
3. Add ginger, turmeric, florets, salt, water, and the rest of the coconut milk.
4. Simmer for an hour. Stir occasionally and mash the broccoli.
5. Allow the mixture to cool.
6. Blend the mixture in a food processor. Do it in batches if needed.
7. Serve with a choice of sides or toppings.

Conclusion

Thank you again for getting this guide.

If you found this guide helpful, please take the time to share your thoughts and post a review. It'd be greatly appreciated!

Thank you and good luck!

References

Binia, A., Jaeger, J., Hu, Y., Singh, A., & Zimmermann, D. (2015). Daily potassium intake and sodium-to-potassium ratio in the reduction of blood pressure: A meta-analysis of randomized controlled trials. Journal of Hypertension, 33(8), 1509–1520. https://doi.org/10.1097/HJH.0000000000000611

Le Couteur, D. G., Solon-Biet, S., Wahl, D., Cogger, V. C., Willcox, B. J., Willcox, D. C., Raubenheimer, D., & Simpson, S. J. (2016). New Horizons: Dietary protein, ageing and the Okinawan ratio. Age and Ageing, 45(4), 443–447. https://doi.org/10.1093/ageing/afw069

Life expectancy by country | infoplease. (n.d.). Retrieved April 8, 2023, from https://www.infoplease.com/world-statistics/health-and-social-statistics/life-expectancy-by-country

Mente, A., O'Donnell, M., Rangarajan, S., Dagenais, G., Lear, S., McQueen, M., Diaz, R., Avezum, A., Lopez-Jaramillo, P., Lanas, F., Li, W., Lu, Y., Yi, S., Rensheng, L., Iqbal, R., Mony, P., Yusuf, R., Yusoff, K., Szuba, A., … Yusuf, S. (2016). Associations of urinary sodium excretion with cardiovascular events in individuals with and without hypertension: A pooled analysis of data from four studies. The Lancet, 388(10043), 465–475. https://doi.org/10.1016/S0140-6736(16)30467-6

Messina, M. (2016). Soy and health update: Evaluation of the clinical and epidemiologic literature. Nutrients, 8(12), 754. https://doi.org/10.3390/nu8120754

Mofa: Okinawa: Industry(Agriculture / fisheries)(Kyushu-okinawa summit 2000). (n.d.). Retrieved April 8, 2023, from https://www.mofa.go.jp/policy/economy/summit/2000/outline/eng/okinawa/oki0201.html

Mofa: Okinawa: Industry(Manufacturing / tourism)(Kyushu-okinawa summit 2000). (n.d.). Retrieved April 8, 2023, from https://www.mofa.go.jp/policy/economy/summit/2000/outline/eng/okinawa/oki0202.html

Montgomery, K. S. (2003). Soy protein. The Journal of Perinatal Education, 12(3), 42–45. https://doi.org/10.1624/105812403X106946

Núñez-Córdoba, J. M., & Martínez-González, M. A. (2011). Antioxidant vitamins and cardiovascular disease. Current Topics in Medicinal Chemistry, 11(14), 1861–1869. https://doi.org/10.2174/156802611796235143

Prasad, K. N., Wu, M., & Bondy, S. C. (2017). Telomere shortening during aging: Attenuation by antioxidants and anti-inflammatory agents. Mechanisms of Ageing and Development, 164, 61–66. https://doi.org/10.1016/j.mad.2017.04.004

Rizzoli, R. (2014). Dairy products, yogurts, and bone health,,. The American Journal of Clinical Nutrition, 99(5), 1256S-1262S. https://doi.org/10.3945/ajcn.113.073056

Rodriguez-Casado, A. (2016). The health potential of fruits and vegetables phytochemicals: Notable examples. Critical Reviews in Food Science and Nutrition, 56(7), 1097–1107. https://doi.org/10.1080/10408398.2012.755149

Sergiev, P. V., Dontsova, O. A., & Berezkin, G. V. (2015). Theories of aging: An ever-evolving field. Acta Naturae, 7(1), 9–18. https://www.ncbi.nlm.nih.gov/pmc/articles/PMC4410392/

Song, Y., Cook, N. R., Albert, C. M., Van Denburgh, M., & Manson, J. E. (2009). Effects of vitamins C and E and β-carotene on the risk of type 2 diabetes in women at high risk of cardiovascular disease: A randomized controlled trial. The American Journal of Clinical Nutrition, 90(2), 429–437. https://doi.org/10.3945/ajcn.2009.27491

Tucker, L. A. (2017). Consumption of nuts and seeds and telomere length in 5,582 men and women of the National Health and Nutrition Examination Survey (Nhanes). The Journal of Nutrition, Health & Aging, 21(3), 233–240. https://doi.org/10.1007/s12603-017-0876-5

Willcox, B. J., & Willcox, D. C. (2013). Caloric restriction, caloric restriction mimetics, and healthy aging in Okinawa: Controversies and clinical implications. Current Opinion in Clinical Nutrition and Metabolic Care, 1. https://doi.org/10.1097/MCO.0000000000000019

Willcox, D. C., Scapagnini, G., & Willcox, B. J. (2014). Healthy aging diets other than the Mediterranean: A focus on the Okinawan diet. Mechanisms of Ageing and Development, 136–137, 148–162. https://doi.org/10.1016/j.mad.2014.01.002

Willcox, D. C., Willcox, B. J., Hsueh, W.-C., & Suzuki, M. (2006). Genetic determinants of exceptional human longevity: Insights from the Okinawa Centenarian Study. AGE, 28(4), 313–332. https://doi.org/10.1007/s11357-006-9020-x

Willcox, D. C., Willcox, B. J., Todoriki, H., & Suzuki, M. (2009). The okinawan diet: Health implications of a low-calorie, nutrient-dense, antioxidant-rich dietary pattern low in glycemic load. Journal of the American College of Nutrition, 28(sup4), 500S-516S. https://doi.org/10.1080/07315724.2009.10718117